Nephi Makes a Boat

written by Tiffany Thomas
illustrated by Nikki Casassa

CFI · An imprint of Cedar Fort, Inc. · Springville, Utah

HARD WORDS:
cross, storm, tied, sorry

PARENT TIP: Have your child read out loud, even if they can read all of the words by themselves.

Lehi and his sons are at the sea.

God says to
cross the sea.

God tells Nephi how
to make a boat.

Nephi's brothers
get mad.

God helps Nephi be safe.

Nephi's brothers
help make the boat.

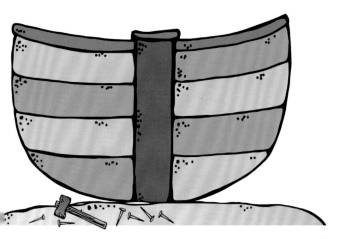

Lehi and his sons cross the sea.

Nephi's brothers are bad,
so God sends a storm.

Nephi is tied up
but God helps
him get out.

Nephi's brothers say
they are sorry.

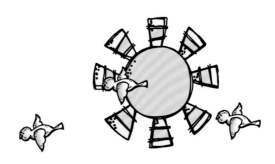

God ends the storm.

The end.

ISBN 13: 978-1-4621-4337-5

Published by CFI, an imprint of Cedar Fort, Inc. • 2373 W. 700 S., Suite 100, Springville, UT 84663
Distributed by Cedar Fort, Inc., www.cedarfort.com

Cover design and interior layout design by Shawnda T. Craig
Cover design © 2022 Cedar Fort, Inc.
Printed in China • Printed on acid-free paper
10 9 8 7 6 5 4 3 2 1